For my mommy
Mireille
Anthony & Amanda
love you always

Introduction

I wrote these poems over the course of several days. They poured out of me—heartfelt and raw. I hope that hearing my stories will help others. Sharing our experiences and knowing we are not alone is important. It's also liberating to take my hidden truths and send them out into the world—to accept myself.

Let me share with you my story,
Years that have unfolded—
My life.

Let me lighten my sorrow,
Tale by tale,
Until you know—
You're not alone.

Let me hold up a mirror,
Let me see
All the pieces,
All the parts—
I do exist.

The eyes of a child
See what the heart sees,
Know what the heart knows:
Understand.

Words might escape me
But the feeling in my blood,
My bones,
I can't ignore.

Our lives are built on Quicksand,
A never-ending Earthquake,
A Torrent of Turmoil
that never ends.

I learn to cower in fear,
Hide from the unknown,
Never trust that you
will never go,
Wonder always if one day
You will abandon
Unintended burdens,
Broken dreams,
Dashed hopes, and the life
you made together
that bleeds us dry.

The lessons life teaches
at a young age
are the worst.

They seep beneath your skin,
Taint you,
Slowly sowing
your demise—
Silent, unseen, unknowing.

Firmly rooted in self-hatred
Festering quietly
beneath the surface—
Now full grown.

How did I know
I was beneath you?
How did I learn?
How did I grow
to understand myself,
A lowly occupant of a
Ruthless skyscraper
Built on a rigid foundation
of hate?

The lessons life teaches
at a young age
are the worst.

Despite battles and knowledge,
Reflection and learning
They remain—
too deeply embedded to erase.

I was a blind child
simply striving
to survive.

I believed
all the words
you spoke to me,
Truths
I never thought
to question—
Reality.

I absorbed
all your Rights,
Feared
all your Wrongs.

I stayed within the lines
I never strayed.
Scared to rock a weathered boat
caught in an endless storm
for countless days.

I lived Out of Trouble's Way
Avoiding wrath
but never really knowing
how to explore.

I lived in blind obedience,
Paid the price for shelter,
Lost my Self.

I never knew who I was,
who I could be
If I had a little courage,
A net of safety.

I was young and so afraid,
somehow at this early age
I knew—
People can abandon you,
Tire of you,
Feel burdened and unhappy
because of you,
they can leave.

I clung to you, a life raft,
My mommy,
Well into my years
those childhood fears
Gripped me:
I couldn't let go.

The shaky ground we built
our lives on
always taunted me,
Teased me,
An unspoken dare—
but the stakes are too high
in a game that's unfair
to begin with.

I wish I knew you before,
Wish I could see
a different version of you,
a different time—
when hope was more
than an illusion
haunting you.

Wish I could see you laugh,
Giggle with your girlfriends,
Smile shyly to admirers—
Peacefully glow.

I study black and white photos,
I gaze in your eyes,
I try to feel the beauty you had
before our time,
before life's promises
turned to darkened
Lies,
before your dreams shattered around you—
before our demise.

Sometimes I even wish
I knew you, too,
together in a state of frozen bliss,
A glimpse,
an imagined partnered life—
A hopeless dream.

The world is made up
of jagged edges,
Always tip toe,
Corners will cut you—
Be alert.

Take tiny footsteps,
Tread lightly,
Make no noise.

Cower in shadows,
Veiled by darkness,
Remain unseen.

Only on the fringes,
Peripheral existence
Invisibly listen—
Others live.

You were at sea,
three little anchors
Floating and drowning,
Keeping you whole
All the while
Pulling apart at
Your life.

My heart breaks
When I imagine you,
Mommy,
In a foreign world—
Lone bear,
Surviving,
Three cubs in tow.

Uprooted,
Implanted,
Struggling
to raise offspring
in a drought.

You remain unknown to me,
No distant or fond memories,
Just space:
Waiting to be filled
until I tired,
Grew weary.

That hollow place where I longed for you
Filled—
My strength and resiliency,
the will to fight,
I inherited,
from her.

Now I remain unknown to you,
No memories to make,
No space to fill.

Now we remain:
Strangers,
Father and daughter,
Labels and words,
Empty echoes in hollow rooms,
all the doors closed
too long to open.

I see you now,
A doting grandfather,
A hint
of parental understanding—
You know not of.

I see a side of you
I never knew
Existed—
A side you couldn't muster
for your own kids.

Now suddenly it's changed,
There's a softness,
A tender caring quality
I never would have thought
You could possess.

My heart tears at the thought of it,
but really only slightly—
You don't exist.
Not inside my heart,
or the place I keep,
Safely,
the ones I love.

I wonder what might have been
If I had a father
who was there,
who cared,
who loved and guided me,
Provided me
with nourishment and kindness—
who was there.

I wonder what it feels like
to be close,
to have a man
love you,
Unconditionally,
to cherish and share memories—
A dad.

Father—
A man who tries
to escape,
to evade,
Duties of his own
Creation.

A lasso of intertwining
Guilt, shame, rage—
Ensnare him if you can,
before he's gone.

Father—
A parent with options,
who chooses to rewind
Actions,
Only they can't be undone
just shifted—
Blame.

Father—
A question unanswered,
Mystery unsolved,
Just desire to know
what it feels like
to have one,
A father who
takes up the name
with pride and joy,
Not constant coercion—
ongoing battles to entrap.

Did you know
it was falling apart?
Did you feel
Scratches turn to cracks,
Widening gaps,
the gulf forming
between you
before the divide?

Did you know
before three kids
were borne,
you were filling with rage?

Did you see
the Perfect Picture shatter?
Wedded bliss erased
before it vanished?
Did you know?

Childhood,
A giant question mark,
Unanswered unknowns
Abound—
Drown out,
My voice.

How did we end up here?
What led us to this place
of constant worry,
Trouble,
Submission,
A life of poverty
from promising beginnings?
Where did we fail?

Childhood,
a lump in my throat,
a permanent knot,
my stomach fills
with butterflies,
Frantically fluttering,
Imprisoned in this cage,
wondering how we entered
this place,
When we lost the key.

You taught me to pray,
to ask kindly
in my childlike way,
for the things I need.

Years passed and I prayed
for the same thing:
a home to house
our little family,
a place we'd make
our own.

Not a basement
beneath others,
A sliver of light,
No walls or divisions
just space,
Bleak and oppressive,
not meant for
People to grow.

Shame,
a shadow that followed me,
Lies,
I learned to deceive,
Hide our reality,
People don't live
this way—
Pretend.

You taught me to pray
for the things I need,
but years of prayer
Deceived me:
I learned
to lie.

I used to wish I could run away,
Escape the misery
of our lives,
Leave it all behind.

The tiny nook
behind the TV,
My own space
I'd crawl into,
Hide—
Wondering
how long I could live,
Undetected, unnoticed,
in peaceful solitude,
Away from all the anger,
the stresses,
the suffocation,
of a family
of four,
Crammed into an apartment with one room.

I learned we were
Strange and weird,
Others should be feared—
We lived beneath.

Different in the wrong ways
that make us not count,
we don't exist in the same way
as those who didn't migrate,
to be here.

Our backward ethnic Arab ways,
the darkness of impoverished days,
A family divided,
Striving to survive
in a foreign land.

Quiet, silent, don't speak—
your words hold no weight
Here:
you don't matter.

Blend in,
you don't exist,
you're not allowed
to be,
to show yourself,
Just stay
out of the way—
Don't anger them.

This is your lot
in life,
Your role:
Fade into the background,
Silently, breathing,
taking it all in—
Don't let it out.

You struggled so much,
how hard was it
to lead,
with little children
following behind,
In total darkness,
Blindly,
Never knowing what your reality
was holding—
how it felt?

A single mother,
Foreign land,
Meaningless
credentials,
Suddenly a student
simply to attain
a lesser role.

Your children couldn't know
the hardship you went through,
the toil it took,
the days you spent
wishing it away,
Cursing the day
you were born.
Now I know,
I think I understand
Why—
the weight of the burden
you carried inside,
alone on your own—
the toll it took.

Cousins above us,
you squandered your lives.

We lived silently
beneath you,
obeying orders
firmly
handed
down.

You reigned happily,
Adoring your position,
Planted above.

I used to

Listen,

from the stairwell,

to your lives.

Conversations,
words and actions,
activities and toys—
the enriched lives
of privileged boys.

But you wasted opportunities,
bickered endlessly—
the folly,
of those who can afford it.

I learned to suppress all my rage,
Hide the pain,
as much as I could—
Just be good.

A good girl
who listens,
Obeys,
Never strays
from the path,
Only follows
the lines,
Abides
by the rules
she can't break—
too much at stake
if you lose.

I learned misery
at a young age,
Learned the hardship
that is life,
Learned about
Struggles.

I felt anxiety
at a young age,
Feared the instability
around me,
tried to float.

I felt sad
at a young age,
A cloud lingered
above me,
for decades to come.

I had no power
at a young age,
I couldn't understand
Circumstances—
Cards dealt
too harsh
to be just.

Now I know more,
I have grown.
I have shed the toll
of weighted years,
Losing little every day,
So long as I can.

No one says it directly
but you learn
as a child,
there are levels
and places
and spaces
for people:
Different ranks.

Skin
colours,
Countries,
Places
of birth,
Eyes, hair
the quality
of what you wear,
and own.

A flimsy ladder
built to keep
some of us down.

No one said it directly
but I learned,
at a young age,
where we stood:

A lowly rung
to be trampled on,
Barely
above the ground:
but there.

I wish I heard more stories—
that you told me
all about your life,
before you died.

Immigrants
in a foreign land,
Othered by others
on both sides.

I'll never be enough
to find a place
on either side of a fence
I never put up—
Only weathered.

I wish I had some history,
Connection,
however small,
to the past—
to the branches of the family
we sprung from,
but we're alone.

Displaced children in a land
they make their own,
Planting seeds, to grow trees,
to build a home.

We went from
Marginalized,
to living under
Privileged people,
to something worse.

We lost the only anchor
to our hearts,
the only link we had,
Unbroken,
to the past,
to Others:
Family,
in foreign lands,
Unrecognizable.

We went from
Marginalized,
to living under
Privileged people,
to Destroyed.

The one thing that we had,
that could erase the bad,
that grounded us to hope—
Shattered loss.

Two parents,
One toils to raise children,
Borne of their marriage,
Borne of love (?)

Two parents,
One leaves them behind,
Rebuilds his own life—
Alone.

Two parents,
One suffers the burdens,
Feels the rise and the fall
of this job,
Watches them grow.

Two parents,
One harms his children,
Abandoned, rejected,
Unknown.

Two parents,
One pays
the ultimate price,
with her life.

Two parents,
One returns
in old age,
but it's done.

Summers we spent
Slowly getting to know
a man,
Related,
by blood.

Summers you scared me,
I treaded lightly,
Still, you yelled.

Poverty clashing,
The world of your
Excellency—
Your children never
Measuring up.

My clothes
Displeased you,
My shyness
Angered you,
Your children
embarrassed you,
in your world.

Our truths too revealing,
Unable to conceal
the way we lived.

Lies this big can't be told,
we couldn't uphold
the image you wanted,
A mirror,
of lies.

I always felt
I was dealt
A bad hand,
Had to handle
this life
on my own.

The one parent I had,
the one love,
Unconditional,
Lost—
Far too young
Far too soon.

I see now
the strength and resiliency
I possess,
I care for myself,
Carry myself
through the burdens,
the hard times—
Seek the good.

I found myself,
Past all the struggles,
Out of the rubble
of misery,
Dysfunction,
the numbing fog
of loss
that captures you—
I managed to let go.

Old habits engrain themselves
Inside you,
morph into
your blood,
your being,
your Safety Way.

Old habits
Leave me alone,
Finding solace only
in lonely solitude,
Saddened, but safe,
in my home.

Old habits
Entrench me in fear,
Measured depression,
Anxiety,
Almost overflowing
barely contained
but familiar—
the nest that I wallow in,
I know.

Half-hearted breaths,
Inhaled necessity,
Missed opportunity—
Sleepwalking
numbness.

Time flies
on a treadmill,
A hamster wheel,
I'm stuck here,
Unraveling,
Standing still—
No new phases,
Life stalled
Long ago.

Desperate times
call for desperate measures,
A bottle or two
I swallowed,
in panic,
Trying to stop it:
Get help.

Scoured by scowls,
Accusations, attention,
Not seeking but found,
Looking for
some sort of support,
elusive—
Just judgment.

I spend time
in solitude,
It's comfortable
for me,
A little home
I've created
for myself.

The love I found
in animals,
I care for,
Give my cuddles to,
It's comfortable for me—
the peacefulness
of solitude,
No choppy waters,
Just the stillness,
of something
I can bear.

Slowly I've grown
from a scared child,
to an adult who fought
the fear and panic,
I couldn't understand—
it took time.

Years of searching
and shedding
Tears,
Unlearning
harsh lessons,
Coping with loss,
Immeasurable,
Swallowing me whole
until I learned to swim,
to struggle
against it.

I found thinkers and words
that helped me,
Different medications
and therapies,
Trials—
Endless errors,
Hurdles,
Stumbled upon,
Overcome—
Eventually.

Naming where I am,
Who,
and how
I got here—
Liberation.

I didn't have words
for the oppression,
Couldn't explain
or describe,
the course of our lives—
how we were.

I didn't understand
the impact
of migration,
the history
of slavery,
Discrimination,
Orientalism—
a term I'd never heard,
but it opened my eyes.

Here I thought we were
beneath you,
somehow lesser
in your eyes,
in the eyes of those who came
from a different place—
Glorifying the West.

Now I know the subjugation,
the politics and lies,
the motivation,
behind constructs
made to subdue.

Somewhere along the line
I stopped believing,
In family,
A possibility for me—
It's too late now.

Time spent
not carelessly,
Wastefully, maybe,
but painfully,
Attempting
to overcome.

Broken pieces,
My shattered Self,
Can't create a warm home,
A child needs sunlight,
to freely grow,
Not darkness.

I want to tell you
how I got past it,
how the panic attacks
Stopped,
how the crippling depression
Ended,
The visions
of ending this life
I couldn't stand,
For days and months on end—
how it finally ceased.

I can't tell you
what I did or how,
but the path that led me here
was long and winding.

So many days of shame,
Intense, internal blame,
Fear of burdening others
with the quicksand
I landed in
that drowned me.

I kept it all inside
Only reaching out, slowly,
the end of my rope.
Embarrassment, the worst part,
I couldn't talk about it,
not really, to anyone.

Pills, talking therapies, groups, diagnoses,
So many steps,
an unknown end,
but I'm still here.

I cherished the cover of night,
Darkness,
Illuminating light,
in the homes I passed.

Family,
a comfortable cloud,
a cushion
to sink into, when you're down.
A note of laughter,
Love,
True connection.

I wandered
past windows,
Wondering
how it might feel,
what it would be like.

To be a child in a family,
whose company
was welcome,
Not forced,
Out of necessity—
No space.

I longed for it,
All the while
A spectator resigned,
Knowing in my heart
It would not be,
Not as a child,
but one day,
msaybe,
A family.

Somewhere in the depths of me,
Fate whispers repeatedly—
Not you.

It hurts too much to see
other families,
Parents and children
and trees—
Growing out for miles.

Somewhere inside of me,
I don't expect to see,
A baby with my own eyes,
My smile reflected back at me,
A place to carry my heart,
Give my warmth to.

My path will not lead me there,
I'm still a grieving child,
How could I bare one?

Grappling with fate
I have to ask,
What's written down in stone?
What's destiny?
What can I control?

I don't believe in lies
We gobble up as children,
Dying to believe
in a magical world.

Fairy tales unravel fast,
the past:
A teacher you can't
Quiet or ignore.

I've found the strength within,
but my path begins,
Too late,
Too short.

I can't erase the past,
the future is anchored—
This old story.

I tried so hard
to forget,
the pain of it all.

I tried so hard
to distract myself,
Numb myself,
Drown myself,
in something else.

I threw the baby out,
And the bathwater.

The good memories are lost,
to that same pain.

I can't remember the good days,
They feel bad,
Remind me of a past
I'll never have,
A mom
I'll never hold,
An open wound
that will never close,
or heal,
Just becoming
Familiar.

When something really hurts,
When I find myself
Overwhelmed or destroyed,
that same voice,
the same words,
Resound in my head:
I miss my mommy so much.

When I'm down,
Vulnerable,
Anxious,
or utterly alone—
I think of you.

No one else
Understood,
or cared ,
or loved,
or cherished me,
like you.

You made it all better,
A knee -jerk reaction,
My sorrow
brings me to you,
Seeking solace
in the only place I ever found it,
Now long gone.

When you left
I found the darkest place
I never knew existed,
Until I had
nothing left to lose.

I wanted to die
more than anything,
If only I believed
I'd see you again.

I don't know what happens
when you die,
I wish I could believe
you were somewhere in the sky,
waiting for me to arrive,
watching over my life.

Faith—
not something I hold on to,
I've seen too much heartache,
the worst loss,
to ever blindly believe
in miracles
or fairy tales, or redemption.

The world is
Unjust,
Chaotic,
Despite our efforts
to make meaning,
Fit the past
into little boxes,
Labels and questions,
Answered.

I've felt the panic rise
So high,
I couldn't breathe,
Grasping my chest,
Watching my fingers shake.

I've felt the panic rise
So high,
I wanted desperately
to die,
If only to escape it.

I've felt the panic rise
So high,
I needed someone there
to hold my hand,
to tell me lies,
to whisper kindly in my ear
they'd never leave.

I've felt the panic rise
So high,
I wanted someone there
to hold on to,
Forever, not just a little while,
another heartache.

I've felt the panic rise
So high,
the thought of life alone,
Forever,
Nearly killed me.

These are my truths
that I lay bare,
the only way to conquer
lingering shame,
So deeply engrained
I forget until I'm reminded,
what stigma feels like.

I've felt the worst of it,
I've swallowed
two bottles of pills
Landed in ER:
Ultimate judgment.

I fell asleep at the wheel,
Side effects of meds
that numb the pain
and everything else with them.

Sitting in a coffee shop alone,
I had a full-blown seizure,
Another side effect of meds,
Not numbing enough.

I've thought about subways
not as transportation,
but escape.

I've hit rock bottom
in so many ways,
Lost respect for my body,
the things I've ingested, inhaled,
the things I've done
without an ounce of love:

I'm not ashamed.

I'm finally learning
it's okay,
to make mistakes,
do something wrong,
have poor judgment.

I'm finally learning
it's okay,
to flounder and flail,
Lose your way,
A few times:
Fly off the track.

I'm finally learning
it's okay,
to let go,
Stray from rigid lines,
Seek good,
not Perfection,
Hold yourself to standards
that don't exhaust you.

I'm finally learning
it's okay,
to be human.
Decisions
don't define you—
It's all grey.

You'd be so proud
of this baby girl,
Her smile lights up
the darkest corners
of my heart,
I wish you could have held her—
If only once.

A part of you forever lives
Inside us,
in our hearts,
In the people who we are,
In her,
in all of us,
Nothing can erase
or take away,
Everything you were—
You will always be.

Your words in a journal:
As long as you are breathing,
there is hope.

They stay with me now,
A mantra of sorts,
to remember in bad times,
Cherish in good:
to remember You.

Today we made
Conversation,
Words skimming the surface,
Unknown lives,
A tenuous connection,
Obligation, Relation, History –
So much to overcome.

We'll never know each other,
Not truly,
Abandonment forges
Strong walls,
Fragile hearts,
Safely hidden
Within.

Small talk,
Superficial and meaningless,
but slowly it seeps
beneath my skin,
makes me wonder
If I can let the past go,
Forget it,
even though I don't know
what it truly was.

I can see that you care,
I just don't understand it,
and the fear of regrets
when the time comes
is haunting.

It's so hard to know,
how to erase the past,
If I can,
If I want to.

You brought me into this world,
but I felt responsible,
for you—
your happiness and joy,
I know
it wasn't what you wanted,
to end up here.

You deserved more
than Life gave,
Endured too many hardships,
My heart broke for you,
Far before
it ever broke
for me.

A wife and mother,
Wedded bliss
lost
in a blink,
you missed out on so much,
it was never fair.

Guilt—
A second skin for me,
Felt wrong to be happy,
Safer and easier
to wallow in sorrow,
Embrace pain.

How do you take the past,
Let it be
a part of you,
where you've been,
building, who you are,
without consuming you,
Devouring you,
in anger or hatred
or fear?

How do you accept
the parts of you
that grew,
Out of adversity,
Mistakes, made in times
of Hopelessness?

I want to live
in this moment,
Own it,
Without history
holding me back,
Anchoring me down.

I have to capture
the bad times,
Name them
in words
to explain
Myself,
Lay it all bare,
Follow the tracks
of this winding path,
Unravel the tangled mess
of the past,
Unclutter my mind,
Dust off the cobwebs
of a muted childhood,
the lessons learned
I strive to take back,
Hostile truths
and blatant lies,
I find value,
My voice,
but it haunts me—
too deep to excavate,
too longstanding
to Erase,
A blank slate:
I dream
of starting Fresh.

You were my lifeline,
So many times
I called you
when the end
beckoned me near,
Called to me
loudly.

Sorry big brother,
I can't be
this burden
to you
but I don't know
how else
to survive.

It's not intentional,
I didn't dig
this hole to live in
Comfortably.

The negativity haunts me,
Some days I think
we'll all be better off,
If I give in.

There were days
I convinced myself
It's okay to give in
to the darkness—
Let yourself go.

There were days
I believed,
it was unfair
to me—
You want me
to stay
but
I'm suffering,
Lonely,
you can get over
not having
a sister
who's in pain.

I start hating myself
so intensely,
I feel weak—
All travels ending
in the same place:
Desperation.

I don't want to be
this person,
A wet blanket,
on a cloudless, sunny day.

My calls stir fear within you,
You answer
what's wrong?
Not
Hello—
A greeting so telling
It's further depressing.

I hate being
this girl,
Pathetic and frail,
on the edges
of the End—
Out of control.

I'm writing down my
Childhood,
Trying to purge
My Self
of haunting memories,
Ingrained negativities,
want to leave it all behind
in long gone days.

I'm unearthing my past,
Seeking self-worth
in undoing
the ruin
of what I learned.

I thought we were unlucky,
Born to be
Beneath,
live underfoot,
not worthy
or deserving
of happy lives.

I envied you,
The Privileged,
Running amok above us
Never really knowing
All that you had.

Cold tile floor,
Unfinished basement,
Browning walls,
Tall slender windows,
Horizontal slivers,
of the outside world.

We're little mice
Here,
Barely visible,
Buried existence,
Living off our
Meager means,
Grateful to be
Miniscule occupants
in a giant's land.

We're living on borrowed
Time,
Forever pleasing our masters,
Slowly losing the voices
we may have had.

Homework
was my great escape,
Buried
myself in books,
Shielded from the world
by work—
Can't catch my
conscience on
innocent labour.

Hiding from impending doom,
Numbing the pain
of Loss,
Work was okay,
A valiant escape
to lose yourself in.

You see the sweet surface
but my heart's edges
are tattered,
withered,
with pain
that deflate them.

I can't relate to
White picket fences,
Sheltered lives
Never questioning,
Black and white backdrops
we live against.

I can't afford love,
Not really,
Letting go is the first step
to breaking down.

I guess it's okay
we're not friends
Anymore.

Truth is I held on,
too long,
wanting the friendship
we had,
to last.

Truth is
you've moved on,
Changed, or become
more the same—
I can't tell.

But you take me
for granted,
I live in the past
when friendship held
A higher rank
in our lives.

Now I tag along,
an afterthought,
Domestic days
Abound,
I prefer to open
my eyes,
Accept truths
that have been
Lingering,
Growing too clear
to ignore.

I made us into
something
we weren't,
Took the label,
I needed,
Saw
Nothing else.

Patterns repeat,
Dynamics,
Gut feelings
of fear,
not wanting
to anger you,
it's never comfortable,
friendship can't blossom
this way,
not really,
just subjugation—
attempts to please,
well-known wishes,
cater to demands,
but I'm changing,
learning my worth,
not to tolerate,
childish tantrums,
trumping my Self
to appease you:
I've had enough.

I shattered the
Glass bowl we lived in,
Broke the mould of friend,
I always envisioned
I had to be.

I felt so guilty
not being there,
but had to take care
of myself,
for once.

I put myself first—
A first,
Your reaction
Bringing all the
Ugly truths to light,
made me really see.

It's one thing
for me to struggle
against stigma,
myself,
strangers—
But not you.

People want to know
The Truth,
To test you,
make it real
Somehow,
Understand
how you feel,
Measure your pain.

Images,
Scan my brain,
Check my weight,
See the depths
of the bags
under my eyes,
the desire I have,
to hide
beneath my bed—
Escape the world.

People want to know
The Truth,
They need Proof,
and the little voice
inside your mind
starts to turn on you,
Question you,
make you feel
useless and
Weak.

Don't have space in my life
for attachments
Anymore,
Only family
and pets—
calculated risks
I can handle.

When it all
Falls apart,
It's family
who save me,
who I lean on,
can count on,
through it all.

Your life's changed,
You've moved on.
I saw it slowly
happening,
thought I had a place
in the life you were building
for yourself.

I should have seen
the signs,
a long time,
maybe I did
I just ignored them.

I'm disappointed
more than anything.

We've been through
so much,
Known each other
so long,
Time can hide
The Truth,
obscure current realities,
feed memories,
foster fantasies
we desire.

Yes, we were friends once,
the closest kind,
we have seen
so much
heartache and loss
and change together,
but this one seems to have left me
behind.

You surprised me,
the kind of friend
I really need,
Just maybe
never had.

You've been there for me,
Understood the hurdles
I struggled with,
Never expected
Perfection,
or anything,
from me.

Labels have changed,
Aligned with reality,
Erased the memories
of friendship
I thought was real—
just selfish.

Try to envision
My happy,
A family,
A reality for me
I can't buy into.

Have to let it go,
the Past,
that haunts me,
Follows me,
Steadily,
Wondering if I can
Start again,
be someone new.

The burdens I carry
Breed worry,
Constantly,
want to find a better place,
to launch from:
Adifferent life.

I keep searching,
not knowing
what I'm really
looking for,
Just meeting people,
Countless interactions,
Measuring
Characteristics,
Trying to connect
Dots,
Build a path somewhere
Better,
Together,
with someone.

Hard to envision
a different end
to a story
that seems to have
a conclusion
drawn out.

I've seen the darkness,
Bad as it can get,
No hope
Just panic—
A voice screaming
Inside constantly,
Yelling,
Telling you
to let go,
end the suffering,
you can't breathe
or live this way,
unnamed fears,
the shadows that
follow you,
steadily sowing
your demise,
blindness,
you only see horror—
a see-saw stuck
in the mud
you can't escape from.

I wanted to tell you
The Truth,
it was hard for me,
Trusting,
Opening up:
Letting you in.

I couldn't understand
why you cared—
Pity, fear, obligation?

She asked why
it was so hard
to believe,
that someone cared for me.

I guess it was easier
to struggle on my own
than confront
Slippery realities—
I don't feel worthy
of this help,
I survive alone.

You're kind,
I'm not used to
Care,
Untethered by rough strings
that ensnare me,
Selfless, genuine
Sincere.

Big sister,
You've been there,
Steadily supporting me,
when it counts.

I don't have to speak
or ask,
Somehow you know
the little things that mean
so much to me—
the support I need.

I sit on your grave,
Let my tears
Nourish the grass,
Growing
where my heart died.

I press my hands against the dirt,
Feel the soil against my skin,
Trying to embrace you,
Inhale you somehow,
Join you in the last place
I saw you—
Lying in a box,
Dainty, intricate patterns
on a shiny glass surface,
a mirror
I placed a hand on,
Left a print forever reaching
Out to you,
Begging and seeking,
Denying and trying
to let go.

This is the place
All that's left of you
Lives,
Beneath layers of earth,
Something I can feel,
When the memories and pain
are too hard to take on,
When I need you here.

You can't prepare yourself,
Even when you know
a storm is coming,
Soon you'll be crushed
Like a bug.

You can't prepare yourself,
Even when you see
Devastation
Around you,
Falling apart
Piece by piece.

You can't prepare yourself,
Even when you understand
how precious each moment is,
Fleeting, far before you are done.

You can't prepare yourself,
Sorrow this strong
Stops for no one,
Eases for nothing,
Will never be gone.

I sat beside a still pond
in a cemetery,
Foreshadowing my future,
becoming acquainted
with a place
I'd soon have reason
to visit.

I cried alone,
A small fish
Swimming past me,
Water rippled
Peacefully—
my world tore apart.

We were always disadvantaged,
Accepted our lot—
Trudged through
disaster alone.

No footprints beside you
to guide, or provide,
a shoulder to lean on.

We began
a lone existence,
Experienced hardship,
A family
with hurdles to conquer,
A child, or two, or three—
Fend for themselves.

I wish I could have
known you,
as an adult,
Not a clingy, scared,
Baby girl.

Wish I could have
Understood you,
A person,
A woman,
Beyond the instinct to shelter,
Protect me from harm,
From truths I could handle now—
But then?

I was a terrified child,
Afraid of abandonment,
Scared by loud booming voices
of powerful men,
soft hearts hardened
to stone.

My moods held me hostage,
A constant unsettling
Tide,
I had no way of knowing
this was the way of my future,
Forever.

This past winter scared me,
Transported me
to the worst days,
the kind I had to struggle
to survive.
I fought the urge to die,
Daily, I cried—
I felt weak.

I escaped into myself,
Sheltered in my home,
the only place I feel safe
when my world falls apart,
when that dark grey cloud
hovers above me,
taunting my efforts,
bringing me down.

I can't be around anyone,
Anxiety fills me,
with notions you hate me,
and the sadness leads me
to believe
I have to disappear,
Until I can muster a smile,
or small talk,
or something to say
that doesn't beg Questions—
Distracts.

Twelve years,
what does it mean to me?
Almost nothing.

Time, like grains of sand
Slipping silently
between fingers,
A meaningless speck
in the grand scheme.

Twelve years hasn't healed me,
I struggle
to think of you—
All memories were
Blocked out long ago,
the good and bad both,
Breeding immeasurable sorrow.

Twelve years,
If I focus
my mind on you,
there's no telling when
my tears will end,
You just don't get over,
or move on,
from losing your mom,
at a young age.

I just want to lie
in the sun,
Feel the heat
against my eyelids,
Warming me,
bringing me
Peace.

Glowing reds and
Yellows,
an inner world
free from the
Turmoil of daily life,
the noise and anxieties
to put to bed every night.

Nature doesn't bare grudges,
Offers nurturing solitude,
Nourishment,
the best way to
Quiet my nerves,
Ease my soul.

Today I feel loved,
I am grateful
for you,
the close few,
I have given my heart to,
My family, I cherish,
more than anything else.

You know me
Better than anyone,
what I have been through—
Time passes us by,
but you're still you,
Siblings I look up to,
I cherish and love
more than anything else.

I never had
High expectations,
Inhabiting the fringes,
We didn't really matter,
Lived our lowly existence,
Underneath.

I became well acquainted,
Exclusion,
Understood,
I'd never belong
just subsist,
Blend into the background,
Never rocking a boat
I didn't own.

For years after,
All decisions,
one goal:
Don't be alone.

That's how it felt,
Solitary universe,
an eternity—
my worst fear.

You left for a weekend,
I lost it,
I closed all the curtains,
turned down the lights
Watched TV,
Episode after episode
Shutting out the world
Keeping my thoughts at bay
as long as I could
or I'd panic.

Finding comfort in fictional characters,
Tales of lives lived,
Relationships built,
Families,
familiarity
I could lose myself in.

I sat in a corner
Watching you sleep,
Trying to take in
Everything, forever,
Memories I'd need
to remember,
Really just trying to dig in my heels:
Stop time.

It's a cruel life
when you have to watch
someone you love die,
Slowly,
Painfully,
Losing dignity
in the end.

It's a cruel life
When you've already
Lost so much
to lose it all so young,
to never get to see
your children grow,
the fruits of your labour
Flourish
and nourish their own.

It's a cruel life.

We were supposed to
make you proud,
Provide for you,
the way you did for us,
the way he couldn't do
for you.

You were supposed to rest,
Enjoy your life,
You worked so hard
Gave us everything you had,
Until the end.

You were supposed to
Grow old,
Surrounded by grandkids
Loved by a large family,
Not young
and alone,
worried about children
you were leaving behind,
never getting to see
who we grew into.

You were supposed to
have a better life,
Overcome the struggles,
you were so strong
you were supposed to
be okay,
it wasn't supposed to end,
to turn out this way,
for you,
for us.

You said I'm starting to forget—
it's true,
I spent too much time
Trying to let go
of painful memories,
all of them,
bunched together
into heartache,
I never really tried
to find the good times,
they're long buried,
in the sands of a past
I can't go back to.

I remember
your beautiful smile,
the way you were—
there for me always,
you comforted me,
Babied your baby,
Nestled me in your arms,
Cuddled and snuggled—
We were close.

But the good memories
Blend seamlessly into the darkness,
the horror of the end,
the suffering,
these memories that haunt me,
Linger, feature too prominently,
Overtake everything,
Force me to build walls—
Keep it all out.

You chatted in the mornings
while we slept,
Lay awake in our beds,
the sound of your voices
Carrying,
Warming my heart,
Keeping me safe,
Comforted in the comfort
of home—
My mommy,
Big brother,
You bonded,
I felt safe,
Nestled in a cocoon,
Knowing you had each other
To lean on, to stand with.

You chatted in the mornings,
As she drove,
your voices,
the sweet backdrop,
keeping me safe
as I sat in the back seat,
Gazing out of a window
Feeling sheltered and safe,
I cherished those rides,
the warmth, and the comfort,
of home.

I wonder what your memories hold,
What you remember
of the good times,
of the family we had,
before it was gone.

I won't ask you,
We don't talk about the past,
We didn't in the present,
We pretended—
it wasn't happening,
We chose optimism
in a time
of horrid despair.

Even now I'm not ready
to share,
Joyous memories,
it still feels wrong,
the injustice,
it's not fair,
I can't lose myself
in memories—
they will never be
Happy,
to me,
just grief—
over what we've lost.

I need to erase the past,
make peace with it somehow,
Absorb into my skin
Memories of days
Long gone—
Be strong.

But visions and words
Haunt me,
you laid there
Day after day,
Seeing the end grow near,
you hid your fear,
Tried to protect us
until your last breath.

I suppressed all the rage,
and the pain,
I fought against tears,
I tried to believe
You'd get through this.

Your body, slowly failed,
I could see, the fear,
Growing, within you—
It killed me.

We lost you—
for days you were gone,
then your last breath,
sealing your fate, sealing ours,
I would give anything to
hold your hand again,
to feel the love
only a mother can give
to her kids.

They told us it was time
to say goodbye,
You'd be leaving us soon—
this is it.

I held your hand,
Felt the warmth,
Your eyes closed,
I said a prayer to God—
made one request.

I just needed to know,
I wanted a sign you could hear me,
you were listening to my words,
Understood what I said.

I waited for your hand
to squeeze mine back,
I cried so hard for you,
but told you I'd be fine—
I knew,
that's what you wanted most,
for us to thrive,
to be okay,
Somehow,
to go on with our lives.

I said a prayer to God,
the last time that I prayed,
the last time I believed,
Even slightly—
Waiting for a sign
that never came.

You believed in God,
Miracles and faith,
Drew your strength
from a place
I quickly came to hate,
I can't believe in.

I'd give anything to know
What happens when you die—
Ashes to ashes,
Dust to dust,
is that all I have left
to hold on to?

I wish I had a glimmer,
A sliver, of hope,
A shred of belief,
the possibility
of seeing you again in death
somewhere in the sky,
at home
with your mother, father, brother.

I know why
people want to believe
Fairy tale endings exist,
We all live happily ever after
If not on earth,
Somewhere far better—
but I can't believe in lies,
too many harsh truths
have made me,
See too clearly.

I could never relate,
Privileged kids
never knowing
what pain was—
how it felt
to grow up
how we did,
to lose a shining light,
to be scarred for life.

I could never relate,
Sheltered lives
haven't seen sorrow,
haven't had to forge
deep walls,
keep darkness at bay.

I found my strength,
Resiliency grew,
out of necessity—
I protect myself.

I could never relate,
Can't afford to let go,
these rough edges
Borne of experience,
Weathered and worn—
Keep me safe.

I love you so much,
Sometimes you remind me
of her,
in the way you care—
A bottomless, endless
Genuine concern,
I know you'll be there
if I need you,
you try to protect me,
support me,
help me,
it means the world to me
to have you in my life,
there's nothing like a sister—
a bond that endures.

I've made peace with you.
At first I was ashamed,
I tried to stop,
Spiraled
Wildly
Out of control,
Landed in the same place:
Seeking death.

At times I thought I could
Let go,
Thought the past
was behind me,
Felt sunny days shining:
Tried to stop.

Now I know,
Without you
I lose control,
I struggle to find
Reasons
Not to end it,
I can't explain why
I just know
I need you,
and
I'm not ashamed, anymore.

Care is hard for me,
I resist it
with all that I have.

In a tiny place
I may long for it,
Relish a hug,
Need consoling,
But I know—
It's the feeling
I have to fight most,
When it seeps in
it weakens me,
takes me to a place
of vulnerability,
brings me back to you—
Gone.

I told you I was sick,
A cold took hold
of me,
A reason you'll believe—
without question.

I need solitude,
Isolation,
Plenty of rest
but I wonder how
you never see,
beyond the thin veil
draped over me,
the sadness,
haunting beneath,
the little well forming
in my eyes.

I know the truth.

You've seen me cry
turned away,
Pretended not to see,
the stream of tears
You didn't know
how to contain.

Truth is I just needed
a friend.

These days I know
it's best
to fight my own battles
Stand strong,
Alone,
It's all we ever really have.

You told me I'm too sensitive,
have too many feelings,
Wear my heart on my sleeve
Like I'm reckless.

I used to hate that part of me,
that felt so strongly, deeply, intensely,
that cried at the slightest sorrow—
Mine,
A stranger's
An animal's.

I used to wish I could be strong,
Feel less,
Numb myself,
My emotions,
Suppress triggers
I couldn't control.

Now I know better.

The part of me
you see
as weak
Is the best thing.

The part of me
you see
as weak
Fosters connections:
the best parts of my life,
that keep me whole.

Open letter to an
Unqualified psychiatrist.

You sat blankly
Hearing my words,
Judging me,
Barely uttering
Anything,
Scribbling notes
Analyzing me—
Six months
One day a week
Wasted,
Useless analysis.

You finally spoke,
Handed down to me
Your prognosis.

I'm dead inside
The result of watching
My mother die.

You're unqualified.

And you failed me.